Houses and Homes

Kath Cox and Pat Hughes

Wayland

◆ HISTORY FROM PHOTOGRAPHS ◆

Notes for Parents and Teachers

This book provides a flexible teaching resource for Early Years history. Two levels of text are given – a simple version and a more advanced and extended level. The book can be used for:

- ◆ Early stage readers at Key Stage 1
- ◆ Older readers needing differentiated text
- ◆ Non-readers who can use the photographs
- ◆ Extending skills of reading non-fiction
- ◆ Adults reading aloud to provide a model for non-fiction reading

By comparing photographs from the past and the present, children are able to develop skills of observation, ask questions and discuss ideas. They should begin by identifying the familiar in the modern photographs before moving on to the photographs from the past. The aim is to encourage children to make 'now' and 'then' comparisons.

The use of old photographs not only provides an exciting primary resource for history but, used alongside the modern photographs, aids the discussion of the development of photography. Modern photographs in black and white are included to encourage children to look more closely at the photographs and avoid seeing the past as 'black and white'. All the historical photographs were taken beyond the living memory of children and most have been selected from the Edwardian period between 1900 and 1920. A comprehensive information section for teachers, parents and other adults on pages 29–31 gives details of each of the old photographs, where known, and suggests points to explore and questions to ask children.

Editors: Vanessa Cummins and Katrina Maitland Smith
Designer: Michael Leaman
Picture researcher and photostylist: Zoë Hargreaves
Production Controller: Nancy Pitcher
Consultant: Suzanne Wenman

Front cover: The main picture shows a street and housing in Rhondda, Glamorgan, Wales, in about 1940. Modern terraced housing is shown in the inset photograph.
Endpapers: Photographers at work at a wedding, 1907.
Title page: Children outside a home in Swanage, Dorset, in the 1920s.

Picture Acknowledgements
The publishers would like to thank the following for allowing their photographs to be used in this book: Barnardo's Photographic Archive 27; Beamish, The North of England Open Air Museum 21; Edinburgh City Library 19; Mary Evans title page, 9; Format 18 (Maggie Murray), 22 (Paula Solloway); Garland Collection 7; Impact 26 (Peter Arkell); Leeds City Council Libraries 13; Life File 24 (Andrew Ward); NMPFT/Science & Society Picture Library **main cover picture**; Newcastle Upon Tyne City Libraries and Arts, Local Studies Section 11; The Royal Photographic Society, Bath, endpapers (Stanley Nicholls), contents page, 5 (G. Rosendale), 17 (F. P. Cembrano), 23 (Horace Nicholls); Tony Stone **inset cover picture** (Stephen Johnson), 4 (David Woodfall), 12; Topham 15, 16; K. C. Ward/The Boat Museum 25; Wayland 6, 8, 10, 14, 20. All artwork is by Barbara Loftus.

First published in 1995 by Wayland (Publishers) Limited
61 Western Road, Hove, East Sussex BN3 1JD, England

© Copyright 1995 Wayland (Publishers) Limited

The right of Kath Cox and Pat Hughes to be identified as the authors of this work has been asserted in accordance with the Copyright, Designs and Patents Act 1988.

British Library Cataloguing in Publication Data
Cox, Kath
Houses and Homes. – (History from Photographs Series)
I. Title II. Hughes, Pat III. Series
643.09

ISBN 0-7502-2123-2

Typeset by Michael Leaman Design Partnership
Printed and bound in Italy by G. Canale & C. S.p.A.

· Contents ·

A city   4

A village   6

Moving home   8

Houses on a street   10

Terraces   12

One-storey houses   14

Cottages in the countryside   16

Flats and tenements   18

Building houses   20

Travellers   22

Boats   24

The homeless   26

Picture Glossary   28

Books to Read and Places to Visit   29

Further Information about the Photographs   30

Index   32

A Brownie box camera and case, 1900.

Some of the more difficult words appear in the text in **bold**.
These words are explained in the picture glossary on page 28.
The pictures will help you to understand the entries more easily.

This is the city of Leeds.
Many people live here.

There are different types of homes in this city.

Some people live in blocks of flats or **terraced houses**.

Others live in **semi-detached** or **detached houses**.

Some homes have just been built while other houses are much older.

There are lots of factories in this photograph of Leeds.

Many people moved from the countryside to the city to find work.
Homes had to be built for the workers and their families.
Many of the houses were small and built close together.

Some people live in small towns or villages.

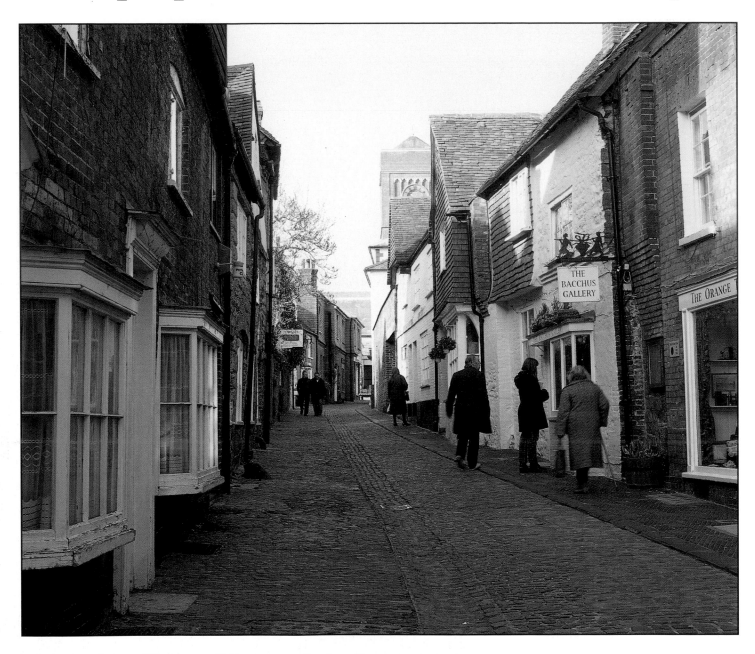

This is the village of Petworth in Sussex.
There are old houses in this street.
Some have been changed into shops and offices, and the
families have moved to new homes on the edge of the village.

This is an old photograph of the same street.

Petworth was a much smaller place then. Many of the houses were built long before the photograph was taken. Families lived in most of these houses.

Zaheera is moving to a new home.

She has a lot of furniture to move from her flat.
Small objects are packed in boxes.
Removal people take the furniture in their van to her new house.

A van moved this family's furniture.

The family was moving to a new flat.
Poorer families did not own much furniture.
They carried everything on a handcart.

Andrew and Gemma live in a large house along a street.

It is an old house but it has been modernized. The roof, door and windows have been changed since the house was built. Other families lived here before Andrew and Gemma moved in.

This house had many rooms.

Houses like this had a **basement** and **scullery** at the bottom.

The **parlour**, dining-room and living-rooms were on the ground floor.

The family had their bedrooms on the floors above.

Servants slept in the **attic** at the top of the house.

Houses that are joined like this are called terraced houses.

Each house has a small garden at the front and the back.

Children can play in the gardens.

There are no chimneys because the houses have central heating.

The roofs have **tiles**.

The front doors of these terraced houses opened straight on to the street.

These homes did not have gardens so children played in the street.

The windows were small and the rooms were dark.

The roofs were covered with **slates**.

Mrs. Hill lives on her own in a bungalow.

The bungalow is small and easy to look after.

It has central heating and gas fires.

There are no stairs to climb.

The bungalow has a slate roof and walls of brick and wood.

These **cottages** were built for coal miners and their families.

The cottages were small.
They had chimneys to let out the smoke from coal fires.
The walls were covered in plaster.
The roofs were made with clay tiles.

The Green family live in this detached house in the countryside.

It was built many years ago but it has been modernized.

The roof is still **thatched** with reeds.

The walls are made of brick, plaster and wood.

This cottage was built long before the photograph was taken.

The roof and tall chimneys show that it is a very old building. Few new houses were needed in the countryside because many people moved to the towns.

Grace
lives in
a block
of flats
with her
parents.

Her home is on the tenth floor.

Grace's family use a lift to go up to their flat.

They live in five rooms.

They have two bedrooms, a bathroom, a kitchen and a living-room.

These flats are called tenements.

People walked up the stairs to reach their homes.
Many families had only one room so parents and children slept in the same room.
Each family shared a toilet with many others.

These workers are building new houses.

Builders wear helmets to protect them while they work.
They use many power tools and machines to help them work quickly.

These builders are having their picture taken.

They wore aprons made from old sacks to protect their clothes.
They did not have safety helmets.
Caps kept their heads warm and clean but did not protect them.
These builders used only hand tools.

Kelly, Liam and Tom are Travellers.

They live with their family in a caravan.
The caravan is made of metal and it has plastic windows.
It has a kitchen, living-area and two bedrooms.
This caravan is towed by a van.

These people were Travellers
nearly ninety years ago.

Their caravans were made of painted wood
and were pulled by horses or donkeys.
The families carried everything they owned inside the caravans.
They cooked their meals on a fire outside.

Some people live in boats on canals.

These houseboats stay in one place.
The people who live on houseboats often work
in the town or village nearby.
Each boat has a living-area, a bedroom, a kitchen,
a bathroom and a toilet.

This is a narrowboat.

Many families worked and lived on narrowboats.
Narrowboats sailed along the canals.
Families lived, ate and slept in one room called the cabin.
These boats did not have a bath or toilet.

This girl has nowhere to live.

There are many homeless people in some towns.
They live on the street and carry their belongings with them.
At night they sleep in special **hostels** or on the pavement.
Some children are homeless.

There were homeless people in the towns and the countryside.

They lived on the streets instead of going to a workhouse where they would be treated badly and made to work hard.

Many children slept on the pavements or in empty buildings.

Dr Barnardo set up homes for children with nowhere to live.

· Picture Glossary ·

 **attic** A room in the roof of a house.

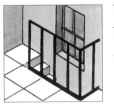 **basement** A room at the bottom of a house below the level of the ground.

 **cottage** A small house, usually in the countryside.

 **detached houses** Houses that are not joined to another at the side.

 **hostels** Places where people can sleep for very little money.

 **parlour** A sitting-room that was only used for visitors and special occasions.

 **scullery** A room where the dirty kitchen work was done, such as cleaning pans.

 **semi-detached houses** Houses that are joined to another house on one side.

 **slates** Very thin, flat pieces of rock used for covering roofs and sometimes walls.

 **thatched** (roof) A roof of straw or reeds. Reeds are tall, stiff, grass-like plants.

 **terraced houses** Houses that are joined to another house at each side.

 **tiles** Thin, flat sheets of stone, clay or slate usually used for covering a roof.

·Books to Read·

Exploring Houses and Homes by C. Lines (Exploring the Past series, Wayland, 1991).
Homes by J. Birch and C. Pace (Look Around You series, Wayland, 1988).
Homes by J. Foster (A Century of Change series, Hodder & Stoughton, 1989).
Houses and Homes by H. Edom (Living Long Ago series, Usborne, 1991).
Jubilee Terrace by C. Schenk (Beans series, A & C Black, 1979).
Moving House by N. Daw (A & C Black, 1987).
When I Was Young by R. Thomson (Early 20th Century series, Franklin Watts, 1993).
Where People Live by B. Taylor (Going Places series, A & C Black, 1994).
Where We Lived by S. Ross (Starting History series, Wayland, 1994).

·Places to Visit·

There may be examples of housing built in late-Victorian or Edwardian times
in your neighbourhood. Local museums usually have collections of old photographs
showing houses in the area. It is worth contacting them to see what they can offer.

Avoncroft Museum
of Historic Buildings
Stoke Heath
Bromsgrove
Worcestershire B60 4JR

   Telephone: 01527 831363

Ironbridge Gorge Museum
The Wharfage
Ironbridge
Telford
Shropshire TF8 7AW

   Telephone: 01952 433522

Beamish
North of England Open Air Museum
Beamish
Co. Durham DH9 0RG

   Telephone: 01207 231811

·Further Information about the Photographs·

PHOTOGRAPH ON PAGE 5 — Leeds, 1930.

About this photograph
Leeds was fairly representative of the way in which industrial towns had grown during the nineteenth century. By 1906, 25 million people lived in urban areas, with only 7.5 million living elsewhere. Britain was the most urbanized country in the world. Speculators built closely-packed houses with few green spaces.

Questions to ask
What different kinds of houses can be seen?
Why were the houses built so close together?
Why did each house have a chimney?

Points to explore
Buildings – types, function, materials.
Houses – design, size, storeys, features, materials.

PHOTOGRAPH ON PAGE 7 — Petworth, West Sussex, 1898.

About this photograph
Fewer people lived in the countryside and in villages in 1900 than 100 years previously. The migration of workers and their families into the towns resulted in a depopulation of many rural areas. This combined with low agricultural wages, high unemployment and a decline in the income from farming to produce rural 'decay'. In villages such as Petworth, families lived in the centre. This contrasts with the situation in many small towns today.

Questions to ask
What different types of buildings can be seen?
Which do you think is the oldest building?
How can you tell?

Points to explore
Buildings – shape, function, materials, state of repair.
People – age, gender, activity, clothing.

PHOTOGRAPH ON PAGE 9 — Family moving house, c.1930.

About this photograph
This family is fairly well off since they have enough furniture to require a removal van. Many families had few possessions and, as they generally did not move far, they were able to transport them on a handcart. This family were moving from three rooms above a stable to new local authority housing. Inter-war legislation affecting local authorities and slum landlords had started to improve the range and standard of housing in some areas.

Questions to ask
What is happening in the photograph?
Why are the people taking a tin bath with them?
Why might the family be moving?

Points to explore
People – number, age, gender, relationships, appearance, clothing, activities.

PHOTOGRAPH ON PAGE 11 — 89 Jesmond Road, Newcastle, 1910.

About this photograph
This type of house was spacious and of good quality compared to that pictured on page 13. Large windows and high ceilings made the rooms airier. This type of house would have been inhabited by professional or middle-class families.

Questions to ask
How was the house heated?
Who might the people be?
How is the outside decorated?

Points to explore
House – size, number of rooms, materials, features.

PHOTOGRAPH ON PAGE 13 — Front of terraced row, Duston's Yard, Leeds, 1901.

About this photograph
This is typical of the type of house built during the mid-nineteenth century for industrial workers and their families. Few people owned their homes, and houses were rented instead. Many families shared the same house and often sub-let rooms or beds to people who were poorer. Houses like these had a kitchen, parlour, two bedrooms and a small backyard. Others were built 'back to back'. Crammed together, houses were dark; whitewashing brickwork was one way of increasing the light in the narrow streets.

Questions to ask
What was the passage between the front doors for?
Why was washing dried in the alley?
Why did some windows have wooden shutters?

Points to explore
People – number, age, gender, appearance, clothing, pose, activities.
Houses – size, materials, features.
Background – road surface, street lighting, drainage.

PHOTOGRAPH ON PAGE 15 — Miners' cottages, Northumberland, c.1900.

About this photograph
These cottages provide an example of cheap housing built by an employer to rent to his workers. In this case, it is likely to be the owner/s of the local coal-mine (note the pile of coal at the front). The cottages are in a rural setting, probably a small village close to the pit. The renting of Coal Board houses continued well into the mid-twentieth century.

Questions to ask
What can be seen on the road?
What is the woman doing? Why?

Points to explore
Houses – shape, size, design, features, materials.
Background – setting.

Large cottage 1891.

About this photograph

Many families in the countryside lived in houses that had been built a long time before. This house is in relatively good condition. Old houses like this one had very thick walls. Roofs were thatched or, as in this case, tiled with slate. The older child's clothes suggest the family is fairly well off. However, there were slum houses in country areas as well as in the towns.

Questions to ask

Who are the people?
Why does the house have chimneys?
What was growing in the garden?

Points to explore

People – number, age, gender, pose, appearance, activities, clothing.
House – size, shape, materials, features.

Mylne's Court, Edinburgh, c.1908.

About this photograph

These tenement buildings provided a cheap way of accommodating a lot of people in a small space. In many towns, they were regarded as the answer to the problems caused by homelessness and slum housing. Scotland had many tenement blocks. Tenements were divided into blocks of flats with two or three rooms. Families would wash, eat, live and sleep in the same rooms. Overcrowding was a great problem. Some tenements were built around a central courtyard which provided an open area for children to play, and also let more light into the flats. The drainpipes indicate that this tenement had indoor sanitation

Questions to ask

Did the people know that the photograph was being taken?
What were the poles next to the windows for?
Why do some children have no shoes on?

Points to explore

People – number, age, gender, appearance, pose, clothing, activities.
Building – size, design, materials, features, lighting.

Builders in Northumberland, 1905.

About this photograph

These builders would have been proper craftsmen, having served a long period of apprenticeship. They wore their everyday clothes for work but, in this case, they may have dressed more carefully to have their photograph taken.

Questions to ask

What have the men been working on?
What kind of tools are they carrying?

Points to explore

People – age, gender, appearance, pose, clothing.
Background – structure, equipment.

Gipsy caravans, Derby, 1910.

About this photograph

This nomadic way of life is long established. Families often followed seasonal work, travelling, for example, to fruit-growing areas when crops were ready. The gipsy caravan would be hand-made and decorated with traditional painted patterns and carvings. The interior was very cramped, and much time was spent outside the caravan, even in winter.

Questions to ask

At what time of year was the picture taken?
What is happening in the photograph?
Why is there a piece of cloth hanging by the caravan?

Points to explore

People – number, age, gender, appearance, clothing, activities.
Caravans – size, shape, materials, decoration, features.
Background – objects, scenery.

Canal boat, c.1920.

About this photograph

It was as a result of competition from the railways that boatmen brought their families to live on board canal narrowboats. The family acted as crew and there were no expenses for housing on dry land. This allowed boatmen to cut their transport rates. The living-area measured approximately 3 metres by 2 metres. Everything had a place, and many women took great pride in keeping their home clean, tidy and decorated.

Questions to ask

What problems would there be living on a canal boat?
What kind of decorations can you see?
Why did families decorate their boats?

Points to explore

People – age, gender, clothing, pose, activity.
Background – boat features, equipment, decoration.

Homeless child on the street, 1882.

About this photograph

Several thousand people were homeless in the early 1900s. They lived in tents, barns and hay ricks in the countryside. In the towns, they slept in doorways and arches. It was the plight of homeless children in London that inspired Dr Barnardo to establish his charitable institution in 1884. Barnardo made use of photography to carry on a fund-raising campaign. He was accused of making the children appear in a worse condition than they really were.

Questions to ask

Why was this photograph taken?
Where was it taken?

Points to explore

Child – age gender, pose, appearance, clothing.
Background – setting.

· Index ·

(Items that appear in the text)

Aa attic 11

Bb Barnardo, Dr 27
basement 11
bathrooms 18, 24
bedrooms 11, 18,
  22, 24
bungalow 14

Cc caravans 22, 23
central heating 12,
  14
city 4, 5
cottages 15, 17
countryside 5, 16,
  17, 27

Dd detached houses 4,
  16

Ee

Ff flats 4, 8, 9, 18, 19
furniture 8, 9

Gg gardens 12, 13

Hh homeless 26, 27
hostels 26
houseboats 24

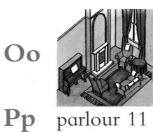

Ii

Jj

Kk kitchens 18, 22, 24

Ll lifts 18
living-rooms 11, 18,
  22, 24

Mm

Nn narrowboats 25

Oo

Pp parlour 11

Qq

Rr roofs 10, 12, 13,
  14, 15, 16, 17

Ss scullery 11
semi-detached
  houses 4
slates 13
stairs 14, 19

Tt tenements 19
terraced houses 4,
  12, 13
tiles 12, 15
toilet 19, 24, 25
towns 17, 24,
  26, 27
Travellers 22, 23

Uu

Vv villages 6, 24

Ww windows 10, 13,
  15, 17

Xx

Yy

Zz